Dream Machine

Dream Machine

sade murphy

co·im·press
normal, illinois

Published by co•im•press
Normal, Illinois
www.coimpress.com

Cover and Book Design: co•im•press
Cover Image: Shawn Allen (Wikimedia Commons)
Typefaces: Minion Pro (text) and Futura (titles)

isbn 978-0-9888199-3-1

To my 7-year-old self:
Is this what you had in mind?

To my 49-year-old self:
Do you still dream?

Contents

Dream Machine of the Decade: Fibonacci Numbers

Maybe you are a poet and a dreamer, but don't you realize that those two species are extinct now?

—J. G. Ballard

Post Prelude to *Dream Machine*

The orgasm backfired muffled sobs on its crest. I dreamed of the nightmare man, flaying him into submission with a whip made of barbed wire hangers. The attacking hounds were dispatched to disintegrate while I remained poised as a bullet bounding off bark. I slapped my mother. I shook her. I shut her up. Disposed of her deluded dismemorial frame. The children! I was looséd mining for grief, blood pooling in my lap. The habit I wore was a knot of slipped salvation and pregnancy taunted me night upon night. I plant weddings. I married my bones, silver needles tore through my skin. Waiting for the bus in the rain, Him showed me three faces not two. I wanted to run until my arms got tired. A possum bit my outstretched hand. What is raw in my mind is the suffocating anxiety of waking startled and accompanied. The ghost of a dream expands, consumes more space than necessary. If I can sleep with enervity, prepare to wager all you crave. I cannot be beat.

Dream Machine *of the* Decade: Positive Integers

dream, n. /dri:m/ A train of thoughts, images or fancies passing through the mind during sleep; a vision during sleep; the state in which this occurs.

machine, n. /mə'ʃin/ A structure regarded as functioning as an independent living body, without mechanical involvement. A material or immaterial structure. A scheme or plot. Anything that transmits force or directs its application.

—*Oxford English Dictionary*

13 I wake up afraid. Shifting to avoid a glimpse of specters in the dwindling dark. Curled against the carnivorous cold. Shivering to sleep, dreams costumed in the familiar. They move the way mountains move through mist. They perform the day's events, lip-syncing karaoke. Their genetic stage makeup is rogue fantasy and refried memory, assuming my watermelon allergy is caused by Gallagher. I am bored but my ears pop nonstop.

27 Struggling out of the grayness, pulling stunt upon nuclear stunt to be unheard unheeded to be noticed to stand out in my mind. A seizure of one sense to liberate another. *Penetrate or swallow* the dreams cloy as they propel violence as projection. The silence of disaster pries open my eyes.

300 I stole an extra hour. Bones in my face grimace beneath my skin. Am I awake? I had an angry sister and no car at a chicken shack a Nigerian wanted to photograph me intimately. I fumed cumulonimbus sputtering acid rain. *What is the big deal?* Maybe, something, I overcast I overate finally lifted my skirt astonished to display a glowing set of hiss and hearse genitals. When did I become a semicolon? Riding Houston on the El in a figure eight or infinitely. The trees and billboard graffiti the same neon hue as the moot roaring vacuum outside my studio door.

5 They are marooned in a jar of fog as if I had fallen asleep with the TV on and the vulgar animation was seeping into my subconscious. Upon waking they leave the impression of having overheard a couple fight or fuck or fucking fight and then fucking fuck. The impression that while I was a fly on the wall for all my eyes I could not see a thing. Light pours into the room. The dreams flit away abandoning their sole aural voyeur.

10 I woke up blushing. When I was not dreaming of the toothsome wolf, the ecru fox, the scorpion's sting, the Him, my sleeping world was stillness. Unknotting Him tie. Him tipsy smile instigating mischief. Him eyes on my thighs descending the stair. Him bold hands in my hair. Him tasting me, neck savory. Him four kisses. Him stole into my mouth. Him teeth impressing my bottom lip. The details shuffle and disorder themselves, looping like a scratched record. Surely a dream. But the heat endures. Him, my only appetite. Distracted, I try to redream Him all day.

789 The pipes were flooding the abandoned mall and this woman in rags this bag lady just kept screaming at me and obscene and with a fire hose and with dogs and the wet dog smell left me gagging and castaway in middle America I was stranded and I could not go down the escalator I was scared. There were no stairs. Joan Crawford was after me. Alone.

Dream Machine of the Decade: Negative Integers

Everything in the dream is the dreamer.

—Angela Welling

79 Against my eyelids light tinted aquamarine pressed and fluttered like a stomach before reciting sunrise. In the dark a whirligig so fast I suffer centrical spasm and regurgitate emotionally. The sneezes were almost orgasmic. A boil on my navel orange oozed capers, seeds hatching spiders in my shoes. I was never more happy to be a multicolor horse of the apocalypse riding a rainbow into hell.

6 Do not pretend that you do not know how to sleep purely for the dream. Do not ignore the moon streaming high-speed light into your window. Do not deny wishing that you were not sleeping alone. Do not fear the boogeyman, he is no more real than the lover borne in the depths of your dreams. Do not seek to control the way you do in waking life, for you will only ruin what prophecy you may receive. Do not knot yourself up over the meaning, let it instead fall through your fingers like sand.

15 The sun did not barrel through my window like a freight train. While it crouched behind the clouds the skin covered with hair tightened and madly acupunctured. I told my mother, I told her! Shrieking as she foisted me upon that pussing, wounded nightmare man. In Arabic I, runaway, pitched myself into ditch and days and milk that was spoiled half and half. The best and worst delayed hangover hung-over Grey Day! Grey Day! If this is what you call morning I don't want to know who you would call a slut. Probably some saint.

38 Where my name ends Him name begins. The stranger and the vessel. Him do not want slow kisses. To Him sex is not a question. Sex is an answer Him give. It is a wordless understanding. A laced-up innocence. Him make me sweat. Him and I are the seduction. Him another word for hero. Him has amber eyes of a feral beast. Mocking me, clothed in a pressed, collared shirt. Him has me tied to the stake. Him is the flame consuming my entire body.

22 I was a professional wrestler. I wrestled against Mickey Rourke. I kept winning. I defeated every opponent, all men. Trained in the Brazilian martial arts I was unstoppable. If you crossed me I would nail your sack to the floor and set the whole house on fire leaving you with a rusty butter knife. At day's end I would drink my beer through a straw. While stroking the peel of a straight banana.

128 My friends and I at an in vitro fertilization clinic. But late to board the bus. I was running and Boy Scouts were laughing at me. I stood knocking at the glass door but the driver stared ahead blank like I was a ghost. And I am not invisible just look at my pancreas. I mean I may have an onion skin but I croak out a protest to the grey light hazing the room until it vomits a steady yellow and my eyelids are no longer laser red.

Dream Machine of the Decade: Imaginary Numbers

Please grab me please erase this busted dream
—Kim Hyesoon, trans. Don Mee Choi

i. The bared soles of my feet told me the devil would snatch me into hell. Under the bed does not exist when the matters sleep on the floor. Why are you ramming my face into my fists? I was fine and this dream is a gleaming down the drain. It is a washed-up letter in a bottle baby trashy dopey siren song cooing: *remember me, the fetal lover you cradle within your skull? I am destroying you.*

ii. Was that my hand reached to draw the shear curtain open? Was it dusk or closer to dawn? Was darkness? Was some voice calling my name? Was it reckless Dream? Was it God? Was awe filled awful? Was wasps stinging me even then? Was needing kneady? Was where? Was I?

iii. I woke up damn near in tears. I felt like a startled infant who could not quit crying. I had not started, was stuck like a television between channels on 'shrooms crawling between the walls. All I remember was Him and the nightmare man had the same twisted, burned-down blackface. As I stumbled to the surface of consciousness the last thing—the first thing—after gasping awake—no. The images are chained to that man's land, the elephant graveyard of my brain. The cling-to, the dried marrow in the bones suckling what is already anemic. I am not your melancholy baby or an atomic sex bomb ready to demolish God's spoiled children. In a swooping fell my mood. My rare sapphire sickled into soul. My beat is splintered. I walk on shards leafing a loping trail of sap and blood.

Star shot across the sky. Flakes of ash escaped the fire landing on garments. Fireflies flashed like traffic light key lime pie. Beer bottles tip over. A glassy classy noise on the rocks. The constellations prize their disdain bestowing enough light to be a marvel but taking their sweet unsynchronized time. Feel nothing but the stoked blaze on skin.

iiiii. In Kansas or Nebraska there are pure salt-of-the-earth vaginas. In a place like Houston the bedazzled vaginas glitter gaudy but you feel them pressed against your back before you see them. The wet rope through the camel's eye. The lymph pencil in the ear. And if there is tongue or teeth involved, the forecast is clear. Humidity will flirt with your mouth. And if your feet leave the ground, you just know.

iiiiii. This time in the subway, huddled with the puddles and all the leakage and the dripping. Like a cave. Like vaginal. Like this is how we are born. Like this is how I will die. Invisible except to the strung out ebony pearl masturbatory sleepwalker. Stale urine, crammed saltines, butt juice tepid. Vermont was still in my shoes mangled with the New York rain. And I never dried under the turquoise and purple stained class of passengers until Joy smiled down on me.

Dream Machine of the Decade: Squares

To me dreams are a part of nature, which harbors no intention to deceive but expresses something as best it can…

—C. G. Jung

9 Does it turn you on? Do you like that? You've got the best mouth. I like those tits. You married? Please don't tell me you don't got a boyfriend. Where's your man? Haven't you ever been in love? Come here. You don't have to pee, it's supposed to feel that way. Promise me. If you tell, we'll get in trouble. If you ever want to touch it—Don't use your teeth. Did you? I had a dream we went to the movies. She told me she was always jealous of you. I want you. I want you still. I love you. Don't you need love too? Unless you don't want to be loved. Can I call you sometime? I can't get your number? What's your name baby? Stuck up bitch. Fat bitch. What if I told you I desired you a different way?

16 I can only access the thrill outside of my body. Hovering above myself, an inch away from my skin. I feel tides building inside starting low smashing against. Again the quickening crescendos. Smoothing the hair from my face until I only utter, until my lashes kiss. I have to leave my skin for this vague tension and every time dying. I manipulate the strings but it is never I who

25 Double fisting microphones on stage, wobbling a little. Breadth, a neon cock. That is all she wrought and do not forget it motherfucker. Fifteen left steps always to the third floor and or the rooftop fireworks that need to be lit with your smile. Cawfee crew cruise, Cheshire bronze tea cups cracking like sunburned skin off your nose, shaken like a baby.

36 Him snuck in and turned my entire home upside down. The floor plan was flattened, mashed up. The staircase exposed like bones picked over by vultures. All the contents of the closets spilled out spilled over into view. The packaged meats, the curdled tofu, the refuse, the debris and the telltale urine staining the air. Him had to slide along the wall. Amorphous indigo pods of humanity. Thick and slippery swallow labia. Him tore apart the rooms for a resolution. I don't know how Him got in. With the chain over the door I turned away even.

49 Husked-out hornets are falling out of trees. Damn unicorn gorging on cucumbers and tiger lilies. Watered down grape cocktail in a mason jar weighing down napkins splotched with schizophrenic script. I'm packing you, possession, on the front porch. You have a big ass for an old man and too much subjunctive protohipster imperforated earlobes. Spread your lids. You have to open your eyes sometime.

64 I am stalking you. After work you catch a bus to Jackson and when you get under the rude lights of the casino marquee you blush a golden beet pink. You place your beanie babies atop the slot machine. They emit a dead-spin plasticity. Happy and poorer than you might think. Aubergine cotton candy hair crawling out of a casket. Death is a deal breaker, full of loud melancholy ricocheting off tabernacles. I cannot stand to be away from you but I cannot absolve you of your sins. I am sorry.

Dream Machine of the Decade: Biblical Numbers

For dreams have led many astray, and those who believed in them have perished.

—Sirach 34:7

3 Not long after I failed remedial self obliteration, vomiting the pink bubbly bicarbonate soul I'd gobbled, walking off the wait. Seduced by the space, it was all so green and gestalt. I traveled through mimetic brambles and mud. Climbing up I stooped to gasp and wavered on the edge of a cliff. Springs of marbled fur were leaping off it. In the lushness I heard a bird sing. An iridescent Technicolor dreambird, decentering my cones and rods.

7 My tongue clitori swell with tart mayonnaise. The fuzz of the kiwi cemented to my mouth roof. The cow entrails taste like kerosene. I choke down the rum and the silicone pork. The fork punctures a boil on my gums and influenza gushes into my cavities. Suitors bring me quail eggs and sea turtles for stew, mashed peas for the bouillabaisse. But my appetite grows dusty and I long for singing wheat grass and frog legs.

40 I watched Him feed some skank sugar in a low lit pupusería. Him rested the spoon on her black lips. Him chuckled when she choked. I watched Him ride a bike up to the curb and start to walk me homeward. We didn't say nothing. But once we reached my stoop Him went wild. Him thrashed apart my garden. Him tore my onions out of the ground. The air swarmed with their dog whistle wails. I could only stand there, weeping and sniffling for my bulbous loves.

12 I was married to my best friend. We lived in a small house. Trees in the backyard. Vandals had broken our kitchen window. It was the perfect window, right over the kitchen sink, with birds feeding and herbs in boxes. I called my mother, upset. I don't know why. I never call her for anything. She said, *don't worry baby, I'll find out who*. I started to run. What was I running for? The film was black and white at this point and I ran through stop sign after stop sign, through a marathon, through so many trees. Nothing. Suddenly saturation and halt. Then my mother was there across the street, holding Sonic and Tails by the scruffs of their necks. They had broken my window? And my mother was dressed like Xena wielding Thor's hammer. Yes. Then she oversaw the repair.

33 Humming to black and white British people. Projected optic maroon angels pinching your sideburned sunburned love handle. Do the French inhale for me and peel the camel hair shirt from the exquisite corpse of charity. Impressionistic and impressed, I am under every street light, shooting cannonballs of fleeting fireflies, carouseling at three thirty. Envy is an umbrella against a sandstorm of affection. You rest somewhere between queue and ewe, savagely pretentious, retrieving letters from the recycled rubble.

490 Reaching scarce contrails. Outsmart Hansel in the low slack grim miles. Try for a caustic coup and do callous hiccups. Nada on the quay or to sea the same day. Armageddon banjo tunnel camper parlors annoy me so braid your heaters putz. Ten dimes inzone the terse rapport. Malaise is a tart archaic bomber haze saying lean me. Furry, cabbie, or seamen there's no queerer dose than mad reason. Los Angelo's sun lows a tropial marsupial toss salad. All horses major in Kato rummaking. Pay Crystal a kiln haberdasher. Collard porn ads laud all adults dusting yore. Eeyore totally can't sing on cue. A-rod enters Cylon code. Call her over ease. Case that transpiration, hayseed or I do toad. Hey central valet, influence is nothing to be scared of.

Dream Machine of the Decade: Sexy Numbers

And dreams. For months there have been dreams like nothing before.

—David Foster Wallace

Just when I'm ready to forget Him resurfaces. Him tries to make nice. Him has shirts made out of my favorite popcorn. Him room is a tangle of unmitigated yarn. I take a machete to Him love letters and wonder. Him says to me, mocking *Look how far you've come baby.* Him is wild, hairy, untoned but not even in my dream could I leave Him at the altar. By accident we kiss, we neck until I feel an itch in my eardrum eyelid twitches like a fire ant struck me like a match reduced to Cinderella by Him lips tremble ashy wet nursing left with one astigmata'd night vision eye. Writhing in angst just the way I like. I wake up so hungry I forget what day it is.

8 Mama, did I ram you like a calf anxious to flow the milk? Was I too hungry for you? Could you smell the matricide on my baby breath? Oh but I love you like a trash bin in the wind spewing rancid garage meat mothballs and gin-soaked panties. In a room with acetone-stripped cerulean felt for carpet I strangle you but you won't die. You're the queen of the penis pendulum. You're a pseudoxenophile with your porcupine prison warden and your nylon merkin. If only I was brave enough to slice open your lymphoma, to vomit inside your jack-o-lantern shitgrin, to push you through my womb and make you mine. I'd have you drawn and Qatared, diasporate all the pieces of you that too closely resembled mine. Don't you want the best for me? Let me watch you die.

369 I'm going to learn to kill you. With my hands. I'll take an ornate blade or a weighted knife. I'll penetrate your throat thrust quick pull spurt slow gushy mudblood goo. Coo my little dove, my pigeonbear. I'll glove you sanguine over my knuckles for heat. Oh you're a treat turkey. Flipped chicken feet lynched and swinging god. I'll pluck you fingerlicking gay. I'll nake you down to the goosepimples. I'll scalpel you. I'll finger your lily liver and giblet bone. Play your ribcage like a tin drum xylophone.

68 The night I sucked the smoke out of the skull you stole the best of my dreams. You woke up and stretched yourself across my back breathing our dream into my ear. A farm and horseback and kidnapping. Adventure and confusion and necrophilia. House riding and samba rabbit skins. A catharsis of feathers, camouflaged lavalieres, percolating rococo kids in full French & Indian War regalia. The iconoclast larkspurn and left to metatate on its shins in the pearl panopticon. Your rosebud thumping against my aster. I have to pee.

52 Kisses cost more than a quarter. Heaven is full of smoke and mirrors. A town shaped like an overgrown pucelage. A fiend on every corner. A diorama of *Hard Times*. Burnt turducken and marshmallow stew. The stank gets caught in the back of my throat with my screams. I'm falling, don't. Let me have my say in this sandbox stomach lining furtive enough for lemon seeds. The porn stars were children who grew up nostalgic for snowflakes on the tongue. Call that LA says the man with the machete.

90 I became the mother pillow, the marsh mill. Oh how they borrowed from my body flaps. I was a frozen flag licking the nightclub floor for electrolytes. They stole the ring from my finger and the mercury from my teeth. Sunlight is blight and a scourge bequeefing me to Prince Charmink. I am purposefully sleepwalking. I love the speed at which your ears turn. I love that. I love this. I say I love everything but you.

Dream Machine of the Decade: Prime Numbers

Life is not a dream. Careful! Careful! Careful!

—Federico García Lorca

11 In the afterglow I dreamed calamity. Never again the pillow princess, never again the prude. Spiders, fires, Tupperware, oh my! To have lit that man on fire. He was a husband, a father. His ghost hounded me through mountains of polycarbonate and latex projecting flashbacks of his pregnant bride. In grocery aisles baby blob arachnids bowling glass Coca-Cola bottles. I was high on obituates. I had déjà vu. I had multiple strokes chained to an Elmo wallet peaking out of her white-trash denim pocket. It doesn't matter whether you're celebrating General E. Lee or MLK.

23 If I lie down in bed will sleep wash over my body like a lion's tongue before the tip of the teeth? Will nyctophilia replace the shrapneled sacral nerve? Will brumous days discloud to sciamachy? Will God come to kiss me good night? Will cauda equina rest against my cheek? Will I find my beloved if I close my eyes? Will it be Him again? Will I tend to the morrow which bares its bones like a black-browed albatross?

311 I put my babies in a feather crib. *Mama! Mama!* They timpani, they trill, they gargoyle. *When will the dog kill the Indian?* Only if malefic visions of the past erupt and people jump from concave mulch bridges. Gather round my pussywillows, I'm going to tickle you. I want to watch you vomit laughter until your corneas burst and fizzle. Shut up. Now the sound of your existence is like a fork dragging along aluminum. I could have aborted you when I had the chance.

997 The herd of pigs and civil war general chased me into the concentration camp. I hate modern art. I found the camps immoral hills of dead eyes. The refusal to dignify them with a burial is to piss in the face of crucified Christ. What if their names were written in elephant dung across the Atacama? What if I rubbed your face in it? What if I fondled your eleven-year-old breasts at the kitchen sink? What if I broke into your home and raped you while wearing a ski mask? What would it take to make you denounce what you worship? Your shiny electronics, your affected personality, the music and art you pretend to understand. I'm not Madonna and I'm not the Madonna. Let me take you to your beach house on Lake Michigan. Make you watch as I burn it to the ground. While I force feed you sand and pelt you with white pine needles. Let me take you to your favorite store and refuse to buy you anything. I just want to hear you say it. Baby, you know I love you.

101 The Fall of the animals began with the birds. They've always been proud. Both crocodiles and birds have beautiful scales but birds are the only ones showing off. A quick fox and a blue chick elope. My boot-flap bruise is sweeting. My eyes sweat saline and I bleed tangerine. Amish glitter bombed. My hands pruned in the sun like blow jobs on pagan Christmas. A disturbing old seadog gnaws on an alarm clock. Higher education won't equalize us. My heart is the Queen Elizabeth.

67 I don't remember how I got there, but I knew that I had been there before. In a New York brownstone. In the room where the wallpaper was moldy and mildewing from the walls. The air was like an older man's tongue aggressively courting my uvula. But this time I didn't wake up. I moved closer to the bed, because I knew the King of Pop was rotting under those Swissed sheets. My second cousin was living in the attic, all hungry and Havishammed. She impeded my renovational whimsy with her repugnant banana daiquiri breath. Before I left I enshrined the archangel in airtight etched glass. I didn't want any unfinished business.

Dream Machine of the Decade: Even Perfect Numbers

A person is the product of their dreams.

—Maya Angelou

89 I wake up searching for you in my tea dregs. You are there. An elephant dancing in a cervical wishbone. You wouldn't stop kissing me. Your hair was short again and puppy soft. I was afraid to cline too close, to moat too uncoquettishly. Are you on my side? I tried to resist being subduced by your honey vugs. Even so I couldn't induratize against the force of your cratons digging into my upper arms. My lips stay hopeful, begin to buzz with finfungality, like fruit rotting to be plucked from betwixt branches.

521 The sky-heavy gloom could not erupt, picking its way through the room I'm writing in. Window is too opaque for a streetlight's single glow. Silence leaves you longing, keeps you voice but I want the concomitant pristine chaos of the forest before the flames. The spentday storm never came but I want to tower over the trees. To nibble their parsley montagious tippy tops. Lazarus ruined, dirt dared to flourish ochre mother's milk but I render the bone soil parrot shrill. I bask in the ashes. I need to be the smoke that thunders. I need to return to the volcano of my genesis.

19 What is this mercurial topography? Why are clouds so queer? Who has been scribbling on the face of the earth? Who has carved their name into the desert? How does a blink become an hour? Are we landing? & how does the earth feel about all this: the sometimes simultaneous lifting & meting of skinned & slick spleened souls across its body. If I scooped up this landscape would I derive ancient brontide? Did all the water disappear suddenly? Will I be able to grow here? Am I there? Am I yet?

31 You came to visit me. Barely in the door before our jonquils joined the musicality of ice melting, ink timidly disintegrating. I take pleasure in the pinch of the underwire. I felt all amethyst and emeralded. I let the silence slide and the damp steal beneath my equestrian socks. You broached my Ignatian legs and we traveled a skeleton grove of prayers. I've never held your canary but I imagine how your innards. You hold me like a bloodstone and I just want to inhale you like cocaine cut with sweat. I keep my virtue close but my vices closer.

127 Him held me in Him lap rocking *How could I ever love a fuckup like you?* The sillage of Him words singed my sideboards like phosphorescence from a squid's suckers. Him squeezed me til I was drowning in Malthusian catastrophe and backwoods apologetics. I knew Him then. Him was a caravan of cadaverous predaters. I feel the ridges of Him thumbprints flitting across my elbow. It mayhem the cowering of locust feeding ears of claustrophilia.

17 Little clusters of industry straining out stacks of smoke. Clouds forming to surpass the sunrise. Fallen branches like bleached animal skulls. The river still pressing, still churning, half erupted frothing over concealed ice edges. The moon hangs around the sky, a locket lighthouse beacon. The landscape is unrefined brown sugar. What is in those caves? Why is the earth so secretive? Time means very little. Who can say how long we have been alive?

Dream Machine of the Decade: Fibonacci Numbers

We dream—it is good we are dreaming—

…

It's prudenter—to dream—

—Emily Dickinson

144 The hoodoo ghosts hijack the dream. I boltupbolster each time. I count the feathers and the corks in the numinous bowl, sit on the edge of the bed. They wait for me, painting as a pastime from sewing minstrel cramps into baked tongues. I sneak sell couths at the ineluctable mirror. I duck lipped the rug with my toes. I hear the death gurgle grudging through the negative space. I hear the death rattle inside my esophagus. The heartbeat rapidrabid flesh about the snapped neck the air couldn't filter into the Kepral lung or the incepted dream. I hear it crunching on my tendons. I haven't been clinomanic for some time. Abracadabra can't save me now.

233 Where is that train going? What paracosmic spatulations are on the itinerary? Do you hear the rain? Can you taste the pavonine ichor? Can you sniff out the lubricated terra ignota? Have you felt the psithurism with the skin of your open heart? How long have you been chromatose? Will this mangata lead you home? Honne, do you know where home is?

21 I clad Him chest in fish-scale pants. Just out of the closet as a homosapiosexual I had a eutony on my hands. Him dances to me across a hexagonal vast tangent. Him blush but all I do is keep my legs shut and penis starved. Him leech, Him creep, Him cheap, Him cast a die, all to asteroid my pumice camel and lance my crass kitsch. Him is a window sigh. Him is a transparent cyanide knot. Him hunts for me in truncated breezes and earthquake aftertastes. I feed Him tuna on sunlit foil thrush. Him makes me feel amputated blue. I binge on mausoleum screams. I lose myself in swarms of guttural color. Him won't think to find me in a clean rote Amen.

377 The remains increase unstably. There is no hope of re-emerging. One only travels further forward, deeper still. I worry over the end. Is it a magmatized core I'm strangling towards? Is it a perpendicular horizon mist? Will I approach my own pupil membrane with a cellophane lens? The waking is weary. Some quadrants are cruel. A hill ripe with dandelions and rock crystal lollies. The sunniest mound. Small girls are raped behind a portable blackboard and disregarded. They play with dolls that have no eyes. Their sweaters catch perfumed fire threatening their stiff spritz curls.

55 Welcome to the dispersed air glimmered with diseases. Crows aghast waterwaysaway to the Himalayas. The new sewageage entombed off the map, soured slid belligerent. Emboldened adventure language shot out naked rats. Monsters skittered their marbles to glue, found Wall Street in West Virginia. Travelers plink and blam their pants suspected steam circled clawed gummy carnival critters. Trumped up wings diatribe. So it clones. You gone behold a moth.

1 I will waste time dreaming. I will confront the broken mendmess. I iconwheel unsteady. I ape ear the spring equinox. I must jail sentence. I wonder how resisting the pressure juxtaposed. I since interplay unfinessed. I have the cameras moving trained any muscle. I clung like thirst. I prefer my feather inside the world. I saw blindness erase the swaying wonder. I bartledbe talking about anything. I wanted the spritely. I feel here. I'm not. I cling to these words:

Acknowledgments

8, 11, 52, 101, 311, 369, 997 were first published by *Action, Yes!*. (April 2014)

12, 15, 67 were first published by *Revolver*. (May 2014)

iii, iiiii, 9, 22, 31, 89, 521 were first published on *Ink Node*. (September 2014)

55, 128, 377 were first published by *Deluge*. (September 2014)

21, 90, 127, 144, 789 were first published by *LIT*. (October 2014)

i, 33, 49, 64 were first published by *Tagvverk*. (October 2014)

About the Author

Sade Murphy was born and raised in Houston, TX. She doesn't have an accent. She attended the University of Notre Dame and graduated with a Bachelor's in Studio Art. Her studio practice is focused in book arts, printmaking, silk painting, and installation art. In 2011, she received a fellowship from the Pavlis Foundation to complete a month-long residency at the Vermont Studio Center. She has published one chapbook of poetry, *Abandon Childhood*, which most likely cannot be found anywhere. Her poetry has been published in *Action Yes*, *joINT*, *Revolver*, *Deluge*, *Tagvverk*, and *LIT*. *Dream Machine* is her first full-length book of poetry. She currently lives and works in South Bend, IN as a silk painter with Silk Creations, a collective of women artists, and serves as the Artist in Residence at Dismas House, a community focused on the reentry into society of the formerly incarcerated.